TERROR AND MAGNIFICENCE

THE LONDON CHURCHES OF NICHOLAS HAWKSMOOR

DAVID MEARA

First published 2024

Amberley Publishing
The Hill, Stroud,
Gloucestershire, GL5 4EP

www.amberley-books.com

Copyright © David Meara, 2024

The right of David Meara to be identified as the Author of this work has been asserted in accordance with the Copyright, Designs and Patents Act 1988.

All rights reserved. No part of this book may be reprinted or reproduced or utilised in any form or by any electronic, mechanical or other means, now known or hereafter invented, including photocopying and recording, or in any information storage or retrieval system, without the permission in writing from the Publishers.

ISBN: 978 1 3981 1628 3 (print)
ISBN: 978 1 3981 1629 0 (ebook)

British Library Cataloguing in Publication Data.
A catalogue record for this book is available from the British Library.

Typeset in 11pt on 14.5pt Celeste.
Typesetting by SJmagic DESIGN SERVICES, India.
Printed in the UK.

Appointed GPSR EU Representative: Easy Access System Europe Oü, 16879218
Address: Mustamäe tee 50, 10621, Tallinn, Estonia
Contact Details: gpsr.requests@easproject.com, +358 40 500 3575

Contents

	Acknowledgements	4
	Introduction	6
	Map	12
1	Nicholas Hawksmoor	14
2	Hawksmoor's Towers and Spires	28
3	Hawksmoor's City Church Spires	40
4	Hawksmoor's London Churches	42
	A Chronology of Nicholas Hawksmoor	96

Acknowledgements

For a number of years I lived in central London, and so had a passing acquaintance with the church buildings which Nicholas Hawksmoor designed, and which form the subject of this book. But I knew very little about them or about their architect, so researching and writing this book has been a journey of discovery. I am therefore deeply indebted to the writings of architectural scholars who have pursued extensive research into Nicholas Hawksmoor: H. S. Goodhart-Rendel first paved the way with his brief monograph, published in 1924, and this was followed by the pioneering study by Kerry Downes in 1959, and his subsequent volume in the Thames & Hudson *World of Art* Series published in 1987. This was followed in 2007 by Vaughan Hart's study of Hawksmoor's sources and his theory of architecture, *Rebuilding Ancient Wonders*, published by the Paul Mellon Centre for Studies in British Art. In his *From the Shadows: The Architecture and Afterlife of Nicholas Hawksmoor*, published in 2015, Owen Hopkins charts the rise, fall and rise again of Hawksmoor's reputation and his return to prominence in the twentieth century, culminating in the magnificent restoration of his church buildings.

Mohsen Mostafavi and Hélène Binet produced a fine volume on the London churches, in 2015, beautifully illustrated with black and white photographs, site plans and elevations. In 2021, Owen Hopkins brought out *Nicholas Hawksmoor London Map* featuring the churches with brief descriptions of each, postcode references, and photography by Nigel Green. I have tried to distil the results of this scholarship in my small handbook, in order to give the general reader some background and a brief account of each building as you visit them.

The photographs are what allows us the best insight into the effects Hawksmoor strove to achieve, and I am deeply indebted to Stuart Vallis for his splendid images, showing off the gleaming Portland stone against an azure London sky. I would like to express my thanks to the incumbents of the churches for their help and cooperation, and in particular to Rachel Jamieson at Christ Church Spitalfields,

Katie Peel at St George-in-the-East, Jasmine Tonge at St Alfege Greenwich, and Noel Gordon at St George's Bloomsbury. I am grateful to the librarians and staff at Lambeth Palace Library, All Souls College Oxford, and the Library of the Royal Institute of British Architects for permission to reproduce archive material in their possession.

I hope that this book will be a useful and accessible guide to the extraordinary London churches of Nicholas Hawksmoor, encouraging the casual visitor to a greater appreciation of his prodigious talent and inventiveness, introducing him to a wider public, and pointing the curious student to the fuller works of scholarship which have stirred my interest in this fascinating architect, who during his lifetime was so reticent about promoting himself and his singular architectural vision.

Introduction

For many years when I lived and worked in London I used to pass an extraordinary church building in the East End of London, situated on the north side of The Highway in the area between Whitechapel and Shadwell. St George-in-the-East stands, somewhat threateningly, in its own grounds, looking isolated, but dominant and arresting with its skyline of octagonal tower and what the architectural writer Ian Nairn called 'the four sinister pepperpots above the nave'. He went

St George-in-the-East. (Stuart Vallis)

A General View of the City of London and the River Thames by Thomas Bowles, from *Views of London*, 1794. (Wikipedia Commons)

on: 'This is a stage somewhere beyond fantasy ... it is the more-than-real world of the drug-addict's dream'. That is characteristic Nairnian hyperbole, but in his description of the church he captures the strangeness of the architecture, and makes us curious to know who it was who could create such a bold, original, and remarkable design.

To find the answer we have to go back nearly four centuries, to a London that had been rocked by Civil War, and then devastated, first by plague and then by the Great Fire of 1666, which killed about 100,000 people and left four-fifths of the City in ashes. Charles II had died in 1685, and was succeeded by James II, who was king for four troubled years before William of Orange invaded and took over the kingdom. The so-called Glorious Revolution of 1688 made England a Protestant nation again, and by 1700 London had become 'the powerhouse of politics, law, the Court, fashion and the arts and sciences: the forge of luxury and industry: the capital of finance: the greatest port for overseas trade' (Roy Porter, *English Society in the 18th Century* (1991)).

London drew in people and goods not only from all over England, but from the Continent too. Oliver Cromwell had allowed Jews to settle in England, and Huguenots fleeing persecution in France made their homes in the East End of London. Soon the open spaces and market gardens were given over to brewing, weaving, shipyards, and tanneries, and docks and wharves sprouted up along the

An early eighteenth-century map of the parish of Stepney. (Wikipedia Commons)

River Thames. The freedom for Dissenters such as Baptists, Congregationalists, Presbyterians and Quakers, who had settled in the East End, to gather openly for worship meant that their chapels also took their place alongside the meeting houses of the immigrant communities of the area. The Established Church still relied on the old parish boundaries, represented by the vast medieval parish of Stepney, and as a consequence was in danger of being left behind by this rapid suburban and religious growth of the late seventeenth century. When a new Tory government came to power in 1710 keen to renew the alliance between Church and State, which had weakened during the reign of William and Mary, especially by the Act of Toleration which granted greater freedom of worship to other denominations and faiths, it was eager to increase the number of Anglican churches in the East End of London as a way of maintaining the strength and influence of the Church of England as an arm of the State in that expanding area.

While Sir Christopher Wren had been steadily rebuilding the churches in the City of London ravaged by the Great Fire, these suburbs had been neglected. To remedy this Queen Anne gave her consent to a commission, appointed in 1711 to build Fifty New Churches, which was packed with High Churchmen, chaired by the Archbishop of Canterbury, and keen to reassert the spiritual power of the

Above left: Sir Christopher Wren by John Smith. (Yale Centre for British Art)

Above right: Sir John Vanbrugh by Sir Godfrey Kneller (1646–1723). (Wikipedia Commons)

Church of England. The Fifty New Churches Act of 1711 allocated funds from the tax on coal coming into the Port of London to finance this building programme, particularly in the poorer areas to the east of the City. The Commissioners estimated that each church would cater for about 5,000 people, and stipulated that the exterior should be impressive, orientated east-west, with an imposing entrance, vestries, a raised chancel, and a font large enough for dipping. The Commissioners, who included the architects Sir Christopher Wren and Sir John Vanbrugh, appointed two surveyors to carry the Act into effect: William Dickinson and the relatively unknown architect Nicholas Hawksmoor. They were each paid £200 'for carrying on and finishing the works under their care'. The criteria laid down by the Commissioners were ambitious and thus expensive, and in the end only twelve out of the fifty were built. The three built in the East End of London were all designed by Hawksmoor – Christ Church Spitalfields, St George-in-the-East, and St Anne Limehouse.

His first church, St Alfege Greenwich, was more richly decorated, as were St Mary Woolnoth in the City of London, modelled on the Roman writer Vitruvius' description of an Egyptian hall, and St George's Bloomsbury, his richest and most complex church building. Together they constitute an extraordinary and powerful legacy from an architect who until recently has not received the attention he deserves.

Overshadowed by his better-known contemporaries Sir Christopher Wren and Sir John Vanbrugh, Nicholas Hawksmoor was nevertheless the last of a generation that redefined British architecture and put Britain on the map as the leading architectural force in Europe. Hawksmoor was fated to be overtaken in his lifetime by a change of architectural taste and fashion, as the Baroque gave way to the more severely restrained Palladian style promoted by Lord Burlington and his circle. He remained in the shadows, largely forgotten, for the rest of the eighteenth century and most of the nineteenth, only rehabilitated in the 1920s by a short monograph by H. S. Goodhart-Rendel and later by Kerry Downes' monograph of 1959, which revealed Hawksmoor as an extraordinary and independent architectural spirit.

His name was given further publicity, indeed notoriety, by the writer Peter Ackroyd's novel *Hawksmoor*, published in 1985, in which Hawksmoor is associated with devil worship and the occult. The book is set simultaneously in the eighteenth century and in 1985, and the central idea is the temporal connection between different events that appear to be unrelated, and for which Hawksmoor's churches act as magnets. Although criticised by architectural historians for tarnishing Hawksmoor with occult associations, the book nevertheless became a catalyst for a renewed interest in Hawksmoor and his work. Nicholas Dyer, the fictional eighteenth-century architect who stands as Hawksmoor's doppelgänger, states early in the story, 'I am not a slave of Geometricall Beauty. I must build what is most solemn and Awefull.' The book begins with Dyer telling his assistant Walter, 'I have imparted to you the Principles of Terrour and Magnificence, for these you must represent in the due placing of Parts and Ornaments as well as in the Proportions of the several Orders.' Ackroyd in a few words has here given a concise description and summary of the real Hawksmoor's guiding principles, and I have accordingly used the phrase 'Terror and Magnificence' as the title of this book.

So, who was this enigmatic figure who has left us six of the most striking and unusual church buildings in London, and how did he come to design them?

Bust of Nicholas Hawksmoor by Henry Cheere, *c.* 1736, in the Buttery, All Souls College, Oxford. (The Warden and Fellows of All Souls College, Oxford)

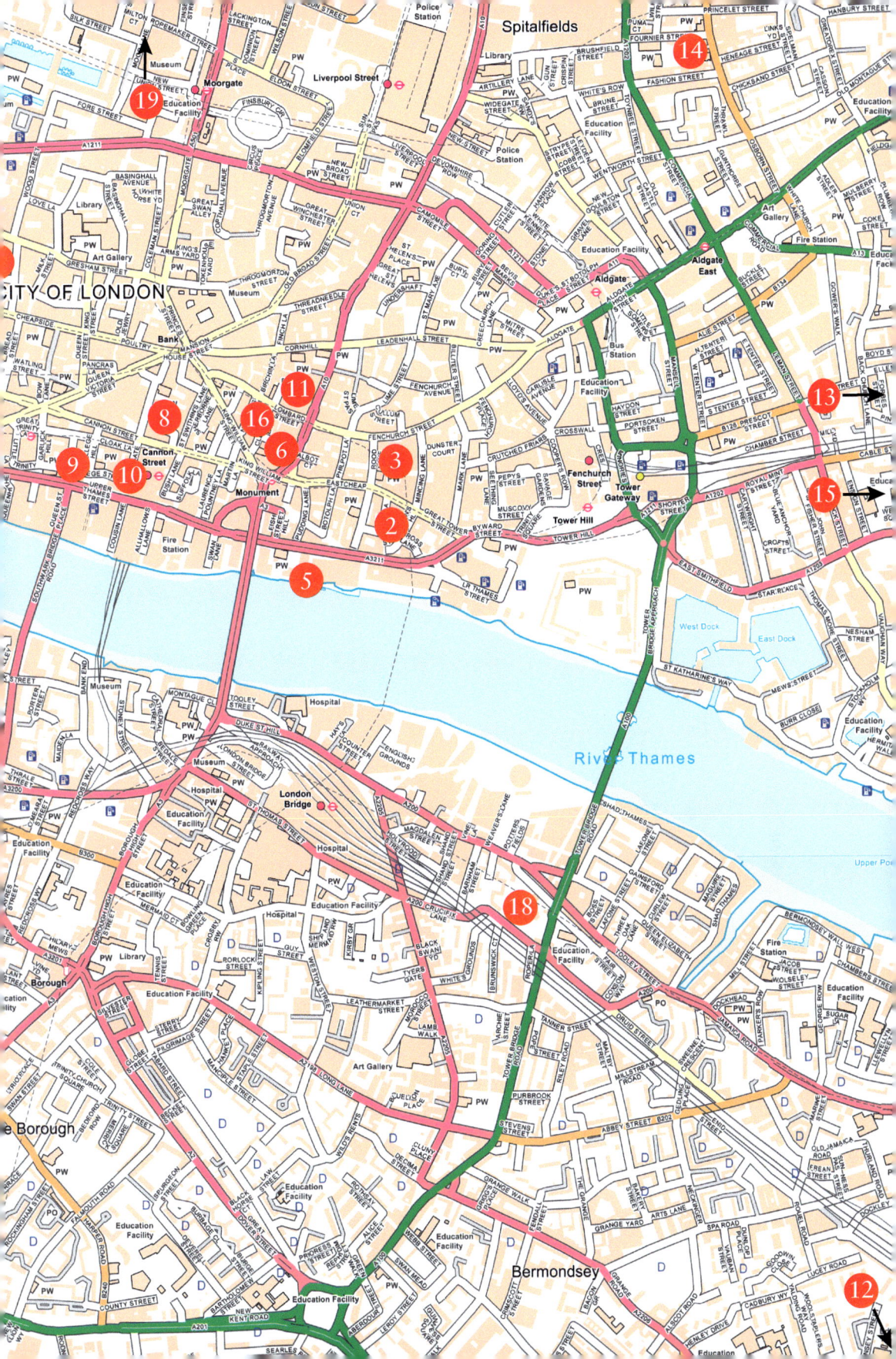

1
Nicholas Hawksmoor

Hawksmoor was born in 1662 at East Drayton in Nottinghamshire. His father was a husbandman, but in spite of his relatively humble origins his obituary states that Hawksmoor was 'bred a scholar', and became fluent in the Classics, Mathematics, French, and Italian. He was employed as a clerk by Samuel Mellish of Doncaster, whose family held property locally, and was also employed by the plasterer Edward Gouge, before travelling to London at the age of eighteen to work as a 'domestic clerk' for Sir Christopher Wren. Wren's personal life was particularly tragic and turbulent at this time. His son suffered from a mental disability and his second wife Jane died soon after his birth in 1679. Hawksmoor must have been both a personal support and an unusually able draughtsman, helping Wren with drawings for the City Churches and St Paul's Cathedral. In 1687, he became Clerk of the City Churches, and, in 1689, Wren obtained for him the post of Clerk of Works at Kensington House. By the time of Hawksmoor's involvement most of the City Churches had been rebuilt to Wren's designs, but Hawksmoor's involvement can be detected in the design of a number of the towers and spires, as will be explored later.

In 1696, he married Hester Wells, and continued to make great progress as an architectural draughtsman. His obituary by Nathaniel Blackerby, his son-in-law, dated 27 March 1736, states, 'In his private life he was a tender Husband, a loving Father, a sincere Friend, and a most agreeable Companion: nor could the most poignant pains of the Gout, which he for many years laboured under, ever ruffle or discompose his Evenness of Temper.'

The only reliable portrait of Hawksmoor is the bust in the buttery of All Souls College, Oxford, done by Sir Henry Cheere in the 1730s. It shows him looking severe and strained, perhaps a reflection of the painful gout he endured for most of his life and his waning fortunes in his later years. He was not skilled at self-promotion, as his contemporary Sir John Vanbrugh noted in a comment to the Duke of Marlborough, requesting 'some opportunity to do him good, because he

St Peter's Church, East Drayton, fifteenth-century Perpendicular. Nicholas Hawksmoor would have been baptised here. (Wikipedia Commons)

does not seem very solicitous to do it for himself'. Arthur Maynwaring reported to the Duchess of Marlborough in 1709 that 'he has two qualities that are not often joined, modesty and wit'. His work for Sir Christopher Wren brought him into contact with Vanbrugh, who had been Comptroller of the Works since 1702. Vanbrugh was a successful writer of comedies, who worked with Hawksmoor on Castle Howard and on Blenheim Palace, where Hawksmoor eventually took charge after Vanbrugh was dismissed. None of the other buildings which Vanbrugh designed exhibit the classical greatness of those in which he was assisted by Hawksmoor. As H. S. Goodhart-Rendel put it in his 1924 monograph, 'Hawksmoor could do without Vanbrugh a great deal more than Vanbrugh could do without Hawksmoor.' For Vanbrugh the overall impression of a building, through which our experience of it evokes a number of associated ideas, was of much greater importance than conforming to a particular style, and this concept became fundamental to how Hawksmoor designed his buildings.

He was influenced and stimulated by the philosophical and scientific zeitgeist of the time, especially the interests of the Royal Society, and contemporary advances in scientific theory, the writings of the philosopher Thomas Hobbes (d. 1679), who in his work *Leviathan* (1651) examined the effects of works of art on the emotions and imagination, and the work of contemporary theologians who sought to establish links between the practices of the Primitive Church and contemporary Anglican practice. The Revd Joseph Bingham had published his *Origines Ecclesiasticae* in 1708, in which he described how the early Christians converted pagan temples for Christian worship, or reused parts such as columns and sculpture for new church buildings. Like Christopher Wren, Hawksmoor had studied the writings of Vitruvius in his *De Architectura*, which celebrated the grandeur of the buildings of the ancient world, and both men sought to demonstrate the cross-cultural links between pagan and Christian architecture. There was also considerable contemporary interest in the original form of the Temple in Jerusalem, which to clergymen such as the Revd William Beveridge (1637–1708, later Bishop of St Asaph) provided a model for all subsequent Christian architecture. In his two-volume work *Sunodikoy*, published in 1672, Beveridge illustrated the typical layout of an early Christian church, including an entrance porch with columns, a narthex with font, a central nave area with aisles, and an apsidal chancel with a screen. This was the layout on which Hawksmoor based his own church designs.

Stimulated by these ideas, in 1711 Hawksmoor drew up a plan for a church in the East End of London entitled 'The Basilica after the Primitive Christians', on which he wrote in the margin, 'Manner of Building the Church – as it was in ye fourth century in ye purest times of Christianity.' Hawksmoor drew his plan for a site in Bethnal Green, which in the end wasn't bought by the Commissioners. Nevertheless, many of the features he drew reappear in his own church designs, and relate to the ecclesiological design issues which were being debated at the time. The plan shows the church building enclosed within an 'Enclosure ... to keep off filth, Nastyness & Brutes'. There are small houses for church officers at each corner, and an outer enclosure 30 foot wide with broad approach corridors on each side, the northern one leading to the churchyard with a semi-circular area beyond. So, Hawksmoor envisaged the church as protected from its immediate surroundings, but with clear lines of approach from the surrounding streets. This plan for a 'Basilica after the Primitive Christians' was in many ways Hawksmoor's ideal model of a new church building, but while he uses some of the elements in his own churches, he never managed to control the surroundings of his buildings in the ingenious way revealed on the plan. However, the plan does show how carefully he thought about bringing together the various elements of his vision in a kind of ecclesiastical campus which included everything necessary for a functioning religious community.

Hawksmoor was influenced too by Wren's tracts on architecture, which sought to combine geometrical principles with ideas of beauty, and he embraced the illusionistic qualities of Baroque architecture, especially traditional grotesque symbols of the supernatural world, to balance the rational world of Wren. This in turn led him to appreciate the power of Gothic architecture, and to discern a

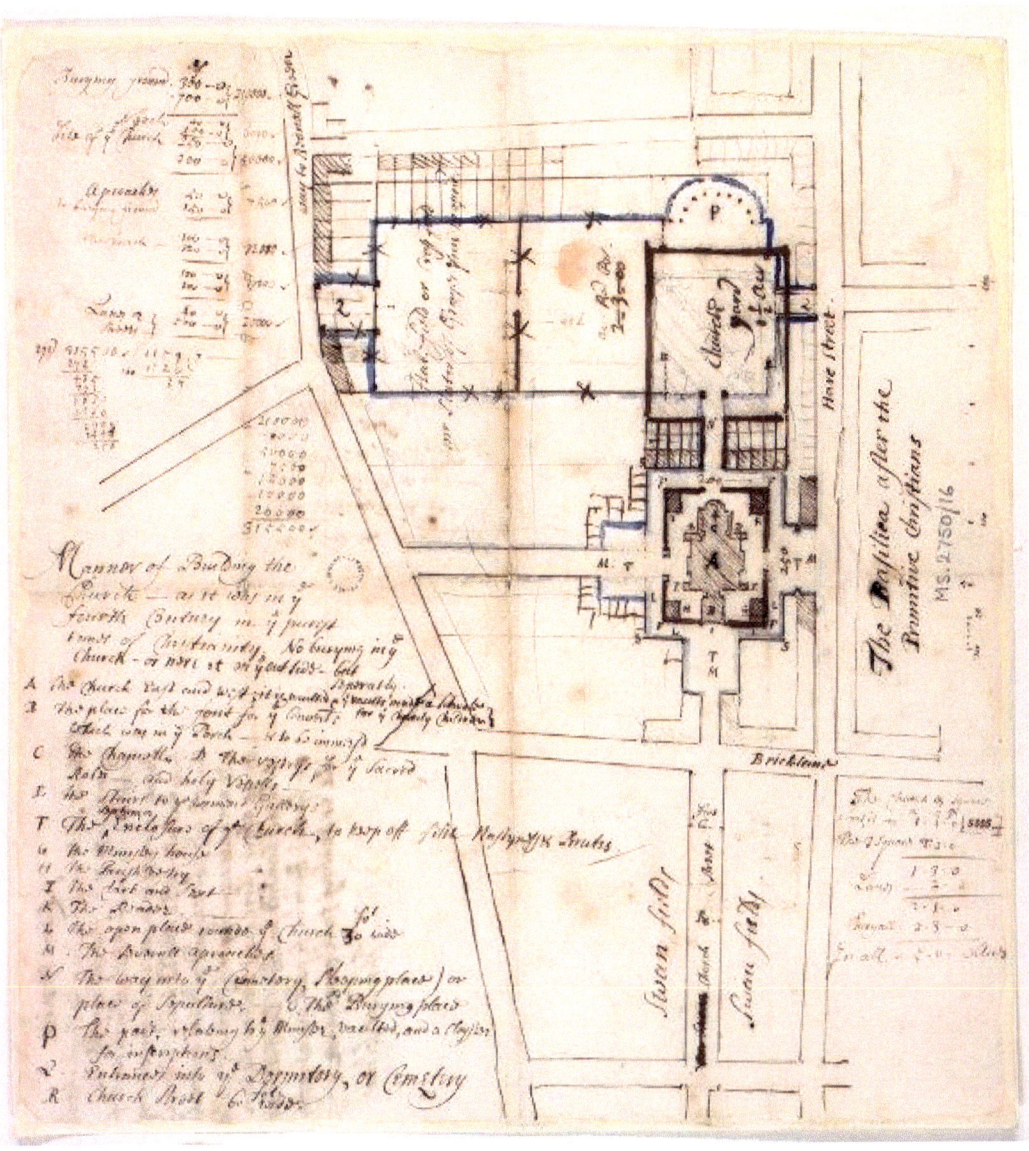

'The Basilica after the Primitive Christians', drawing by Nicholas Hawksmoor, Lambeth Palace Library. (Image courtesy of Lambeth Palace Library)

continuous line of historical development from the architecture of primitive Christianity to the Gothic tradition which his contemporaries dismissed as barbarous and crude. Hawksmoor understood and appreciated Gothic forms, as he revealed in his design for the west window of the Codrington Library at All Souls College, Oxford, and in the design of his own church towers and spires.

The rehabilitation of the Gothic style was encouraged by the growing influence of Freemasonry, which celebrated medieval forms. We know that Hawksmoor

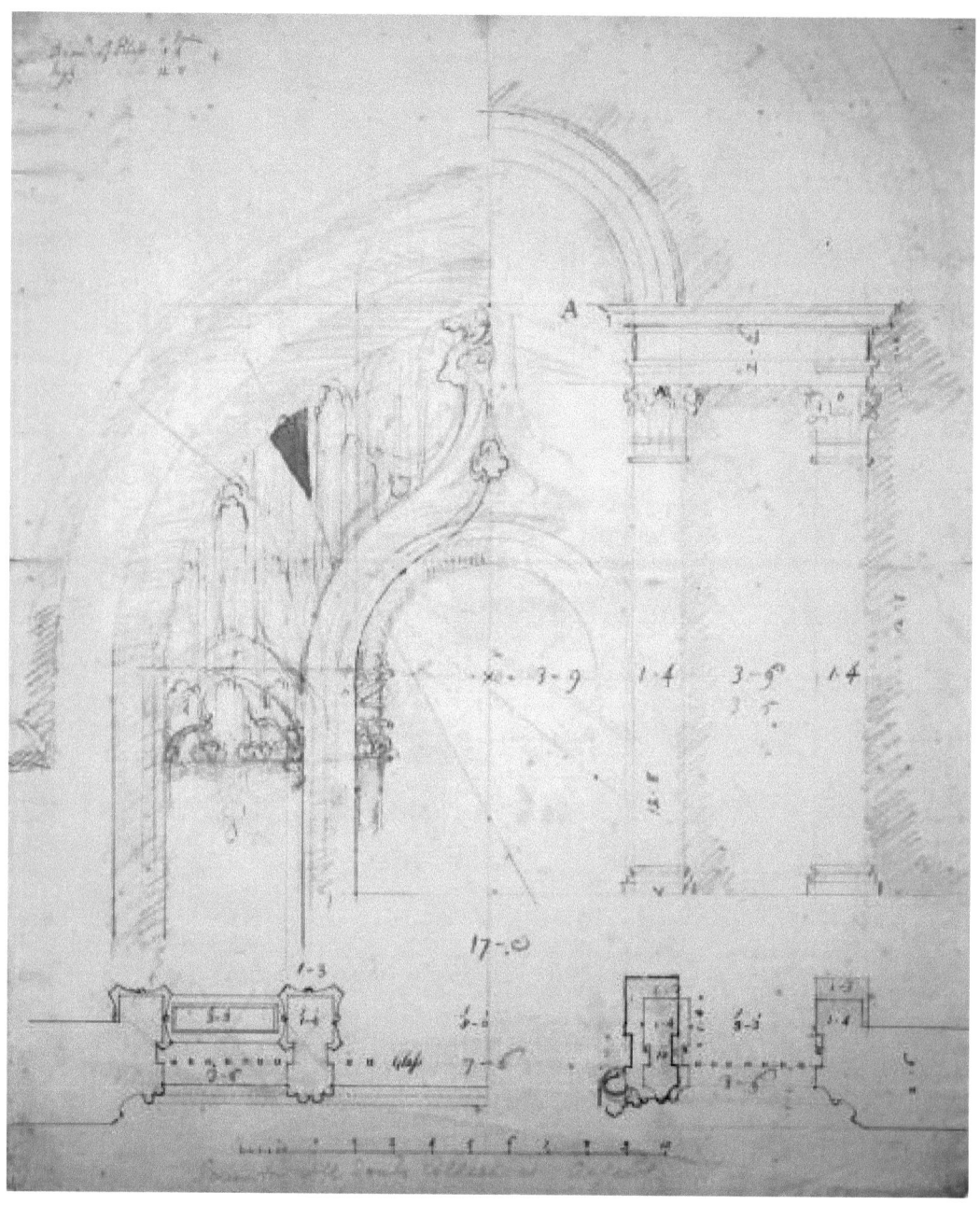

Elevation drawing of the West Window, Codrington Library, All Souls College Oxford, c. 1717–18. Hawksmoor cleverly designed the window in the classical style inside the library and in the Gothic style on the outside. (The Warden and Fellows of All Souls College, Oxford)

attended a meeting of the Freemasons' Lodge that met at the Oxford Arms in Ludgate Street in the City of London in 1730, and his churches reflect this masonic influence in their temple-like forms. His attempts to fuse these different styles and elements in the churches he designed are explored later.

During his formative years travellers on the 'Grand Tour' increasingly brought back information about unusual monuments from the Near East, Greece, and North Africa, and although he never travelled abroad, Hawksmoor was fascinated by these discoveries. He studied Islamic buildings such as Hagia Sofia in Istanbul, drew a reconstruction of the Roman Temple of Bacchus at Baalbek in modern

The Temple of Bacchus at Baalbek, Lebanon, probably commissioned by Emperor Antoninus Pius (AD 138–61). It stands on a podium and is surrounded by a colonnade of Corinthian columns. (Wikipedia Commons)

Reconstruction of the Tomb of Mausolus at Halicarnassus, built between 353 and 350 BC. It was 150 feet high and adorned with sculptural reliefs. It was destroyed by successive earthquakes between the twelfth and fifteenth centuries. (Wikipedia Commons)

Lebanon, examined drawings of the Mausoleum at Halicarnassus, and took inspiration from Greek architecture, such as the Tower of Andronikos in Athens.

Using these historical models, and antique forms, he aimed to evoke a plainer primitive style appropriate for the English Protestant tradition, using the forms of the Gothic style, such as spires, lanterns, and buttresses, alongside the language of the ancient world.

Hawksmoor also adapted his design repertoire to suit the geographical context of each building, so that each of his churches was dependent on its situation for the level of ornamentation used – severe and restrained for his Stepney churches, contrasting with richer ornament on his other churches in more prosperous areas of London.

Christ Church Spitalfields, St George-in-the-East, and St Anne Limehouse are plainer buildings, while St Alfege Greenwich, St Mary Woolnoth and St George's Bloomsbury are more ornate. Just as each building was dependent on its context for the level of ornamentation used, so he wanted his churches to grow organically out of the ground in which they were set.

Above left: The Tower of Andronikos, Athens, known as the Tower of the Winds. It is an octagon of Pentelic marble in the Roman Agora that functioned as a timepiece. It was designed by Andronicus of Cyrrhus in about 50 BC. (Wikipedia Commons)

Above right: The Water Clock in the Tower of the Winds, from *The Antiquities of Athens*, Stuart and Revett, 1762. (Wikipedia Commons)

Christ Church Spitalfields. (Stuart Vallis)

St Alfege Greenwich. (Stuart Vallis)

As Vaughan Hart has said in his *Nicholas Hawksmoor: Rebuilding Ancient Wonders* (Yale, 2002), 'Hawksmoor rooted his churches to their sites less through the classical device of rustication than through the sombre character of their doors and windows, and by the crypts and other subterranean rooms whose presence these elements often signify.'

He was able to formulate an architectural language of quotation and allusion using a variety of styles, drawing on what he called his 'Good Fancy' paired with 'Strong Reason', which appealed both to the scientific spirit of the age, and the world of mystery and the imagination. In creating this playful and eclectic synthesis of styles he wanted his churches to proclaim the glory of the monarchy and the piety of Queen Anne, to excite awe and wonder, and to stand out in their neighbourhoods from the surrounding architecture as symbols of power and authority, the triumph of the Established Christian Church in areas of heterodoxy and licentiousness, a stabilising force in an unstable world.

Hawksmoor saw enormous changes in taste during the course of his lifetime, the decline of magical and supernatural beliefs, the rise of the natural sciences, the growth of Freemasonry, and the rise and fall of the English Baroque tradition. Led by Richard Earl of Burlington and his circle, a reaction grew against what were

The interior of St George's Bloomsbury. (Stuart Vallis)

thought to be the excesses of the Counter-Reformation architecture of Continental Baroque, and Hawksmoor's work was caught up in this change of taste. His romantic approach to the classical past was side-lined by what amounted to the dictatorship of Palladian purity. 'Poor Hawksmoor', Vanbrugh wrote in 1721, 'What a Barbarous Age have his fine, ingenious, parts fallen into.'

During the final period of his life Hawksmoor worked sporadically on Castle Howard and Blenheim Palace, writing frequently to the 3rd Earl of Carlisle about his waning reputation and his sufferings from gout. He designed the triumphal arch celebrating the Duke of Marlborough at Blenheim, known as the Woodstock Gate, with its accompanying obelisk. As the work at Blenheim dried up, he turned his attention to the final two designs for the Fifty New Churches Commission, St Luke's Old Street and St John Horsleydown. These were much simpler collaborations with the architect John James, and cheaper too, as prescribed by the Commissioners, i.e. no more than £10,000. They had understandably become wary of the extravagant cost of Hawksmoor's earlier churches.

The Woodstock Gate, Blenheim Palace, Oxfordshire. (Wikipedia Commons)

Blenheim Palace, Woodstock, Oxfordshire. (Stuart Vallis)

The Mausoleum, Castle Howard, built between 1729 and 1742. (Wikipedia Commons)

At Castle Howard Hawksmoor's swansong was the extraordinary and moving Mausoleum, the burial chapel for the Howard family, based on the Roman tomb of Cecilia Metella on the Appian Way, a large rotunda surrounded by a colonnade on a square base. Standing on its elevated site, it exudes an intense severity that is both arresting and uplifting. But by 1729 his health had started seriously to deteriorate, and in January 1730 he made his will.

His eclipse wasn't helped by his own self-effacing nature. In 1734, Sir Thomas Robinson told Lord Carlisle that 'he never talked with a more reasonable man, nor one so little prejudiced in favour of his own performances'. In any case, the Royal Works had been reorganised in 1718 and Hawksmoor lost his post to the wily and ambitious Whig William Benson. Although he regained the Secretaryship of the Board of Works in 1726, he felt that he was going out of fashion, and his correspondence reveals his despondency and self-pity, not helped by 'the miserys of ye Gout and other misfortunes'. It was gout in the stomach that caused his death at his house on Millbank, Westminster, on 25 March 1736. He was buried at St Botolph's, Shenleybury, Shenley, Hertfordshire, and his grave is marked by a ledger stone with an inscription cut by the mason Andrews Jelfe. It reads:

PMSL
Hic J(acet)
NICHOLAUS HAWKSMOOR Amr
ARCHITECTUS
Obiit vicesimo quin(t)o die (Martii)
Anno Domini 1736
Aetatis 75
[PMSL may stand for Piae Memoriae Sacer Locus]

The keystone above a window on the north elevation of St George's Bloomsbury. (Stuart Vallis)

His daughter Elizabeth's husband, Nathaniel Blackerby, who was Treasurer to the Commissioners for building the Fifty New Churches, wrote his obituary, which appeared in *Read's Weekly Journal* of 27 March 1736. Blackerby summed up his father-in-law in the following words:

> He was perfectly skilled in the History of Architecture, and could give an exact account of all the famous Buildings, both Ancient and Modern, in every Part of the World; to which his excellent Memory, that never failed him to the very last, greatly contributed. Nor was Architecture the only Science he was Master of. He was bred a Scholar, and knew as well the Learned as the Modern tongues. He was a very skilful Mathematician, Geographer, and Geometrician.

He aimed to build a timeless British architecture, and as Vaughan Hart has aptly stated, 'With their very own Solomonic courtyards and chapels, Trajanic columns and arches, his buildings aspired to reflect the qualities of magnificence and order found in the legendary buildings of antiquity, and as such to stand among the greatest architectural wonders the modern world had ever seen.' To which Kerry Downes in his 1959 monograph on Hawksmoor adds an appropriate coda, 'The effects at which he aimed were the most directly forceful, emotive, even violent. It is to the buildings that we must always return. They must speak for themselves. They will repel us or fascinate us, but we cannot escape from their strange, haunting power.' (p. 233).

2

Hawksmoor's Towers and Spires

The towers and spires of Hawksmoor's London churches are a key component and essential for their overall impact. As well as the six surviving churches he designed, Hawksmoor collaborated with Sir Christopher Wren to assist with the design of the towers and spires of his many City of London churches. They were all meant to be important urban markers 'presenting a vision of the domination of the Reformation church over the expanse of the urban topography' (Mohsen Mostafavi in Mohsen Mostafavi and Hélène Binet, *Nicholas Hawksmoor London Churches* (Lars Müller Publishers), p. 7).

Wren had an official house as Surveyor-General of the King's Works in Great Scotland Yard, Whitehall, and Hawksmoor had arrived there in Wren's office by 1680. He was a draughtsman and junior assistant, and although the evidence is scarce, it is highly likely that he assisted Wren in completing a number of his City Churches by designing the steeples. Anthony Geraghty, in an article in *The Georgian Group Journal*, vol. x: 2000, has attributed a number of Wren's office drawings to Hawksmoor, and other steeples can plausibly be identified as his work on stylistic grounds.

In 1687, Hawksmoor succeeded Andrew Phillips as City Church clerk, taking control of the administration of the City Churches, paying craftsmen, liaising with parishioners, and keeping the accounts. When the next phase of work, completing the steeples, began in the mid-1690s, Hawksmoor was promoted to become one of Wren's two assistants, and worked alongside him. A number of drawings from this period can be attributed to him, the earliest of which is an elevation of the Gothic tower and steeple of St Dunstan-in-the-East, begun in November 1695. The spire is related to his other Gothic work and shows his characteristic blending of classical and Gothic elements.

There exists a drawing of the steeple of St Augustine Watling Street, *c.* 1695 (church destroyed 1941, St Paul's Churchyard, London), which terminates in a

Drawing of St Augustine Watling Street, London, c. 1695. (The Warden and Fellows of All Souls College, Oxford)

distinctive obelisk finial with leaf ornament similar to that on St Margaret Pattens, and so is probably by Hawksmoor.

The splendid steeple of St Bride's Fleet Street may well be a reworking by Hawksmoor of an original design by Wren. There is a preliminary design drawing for it at All Souls College, Oxford, showing a shorter steeple, but the draughtsmanship is typical of Hawksmoor. Similar draughtsmanship is apparent in a drawing for the spire of St Magnus the Martyr, which includes dimensions in Hawksmoor's handwriting. The oversize scale of the tower and spire results from the church's prominent position at the end of the old London Bridge, and the octagonal cupola is characteristic of Hawksmoor.

The steeple of St Edmund the King Lombard Street was added thirty years after the rest of the church, c. 1706, by which time Hawksmoor had left the City Churches office, but a drawing depicting the steeple now in the Conway Library, Colorado, USA, is almost certainly by Hawksmoor.

Was Hawksmoor involved in the design of other City Church steeples? It is quite possible. It is known that he was paid for his work at St Margaret Pattens, a classical interpretation of a Gothic form. The belfry stage of the tower at St Andrew's Holborn, completed in 1703–04, shows his typical design features of implied pilasters and heavy cornice with outside brackets.

Above left: St Bride's steeple, Fleet Street. The original design is by Wren but was probably reworked by Hawksmoor. (Stuart Vallis)

Above right: St Magnus the Martyr. The octagonal cupola is a Hawksmoor motif. (Stuart Vallis)

Opposite: St Edmund the King Lombard Street. The spire is a later addition but shows Hawksmoor influence. (Stuart Vallis)

Above left: St Dunstan-in-the-East. Hawksmoor produced a design for the spire, in the Gothic style. (Stuart Vallis)

Above right: St Margaret Pattens. Another example of Hawksmoor's clever blending of classical and Gothic forms. (Stuart Vallis)

Opposite: St Andrew Holborn. The belfry stage of the tower is almost certainly by Hawksmoor. (Stuart Vallis)

The deft handling of the concave and convex stages of the steeple of St Vedast Foster Lane, with its clustered Baroque pillars, is typical Hawksmoor, and the spires of St Stephen Walbrook, St James Garlickhythe, and St Michael Paternoster Royal, all begun in 1713, all with three diminishing tiers of great delicacy, seem related to each other and to Hawksmoor's known work. There is documentary evidence for his work on the upper stages of the tower of St Michael Cornhill; and the spire of St Luke Old Street, which ends in an obelisk, is all that remains of the church which he co-designed with John James in 1727–33.

Above left: St Vedast Foster Lane. The convex curves and clustered pillars are typical of Hawksmoor. (Stuart Vallis)

Above right: St Stephen Walbrook. The diminishing tiers are echoed at St James Garlickhythe and St Michael Paternoster Royal. (Stuart Vallis)

Opposite: St James Garlickhythe. A drawing of *c.* 1700 by Hawksmoor shows his involvement in this design. (Stuart Vallis)

Anthony Geraghty ends his study of these London steeples with these words:

That Hawksmoor spent his formative years associated with the City church steeples – functionless, abstract, sculptural forms – surely has a bearing on his subsequent approach to design. His sensitivity to the visual, three-dimensional appearance of architecture – already apparent in his City church drawings of the late 1690s – was an essential ingredient of the English Baroque style. (Geraghty, *The Georgian Group Journal*, vol, x: 2000, p. 11)

St Michael Paternoster Royal with the Innholders' Hall nearby. (Stuart Vallis)

Above left: St Michael Paternoster Royal. A delicate rendering of diminishing tiers with a circular form. (Stuart Vallis)

Above right: St Michael Cornhill. The tower is by William Dickinson, but the upper stages are Hawksmoor. (Stuart Vallis)

When it came to designing the towers and spires of his six surviving London churches, whose design was not controlled by the Commission, Hawksmoor was able to give his vision full reign.

John Betjeman in his *Vintage London* (1942) describes the London of the late seventeenth century thus: 'Fearful slums, little houses, dark alleys, no trees, no light; the city was half dwelling houses and half offices; and the dwellings spread over Southwark and Spitalfields and Whitechapel and along the river below London Bridge among the docks ...'. In this crowded and disorderly environment Hawksmoor intended that his churches should stand out. He had a particular concern for the rooftops and skylines of his buildings, and he looked to the pagan monuments of antiquity for inspiration.

His towers and steeples were intended, in the words of his contemporary Batty Langley, to 'create a most solemn and reverent aspect'.

He drew on his collection of designs for mausoleums, monumental pillars, and pyramids, which he felt symbolised both the memory of an illustrious person, such as pious Queen Anne, and were also reminders of human mortality and the Christian belief in the Resurrection. Hawksmoor's steeples helped to realise the wish of Sir John Vanbrugh that the Commission's churches should be 'of Solemn and Awfull Appearance both within and without'.

So, there are flaming urns at St Bride's Fleet Street, symbolising resurrection; the lantern embellished with columns surmounted by urns and pinnacles and mini-pyramids at St Anne's Limehouse; the Roman altars crowning the corner pilasters of the lanterns at St George-in-the-East; the obelisk crowned with a golden ball at Christ Church Spitalfields; and the lantern itself at St George-in-the-East, whose octagonal shape can be interpreted as symbolic of the eight days of Christ's Resurrection, a shape used in earlier churches for baptistries, as in Florence and at St John Lateran in Rome. Hawksmoor clearly drew his inspiration for this shape both from the Tower of the Winds in Athens (the Tower of Andronikos) and medieval lanterns such as those of Ely Cathedral and Boston parish church.

In these ways Hawksmoor intended his buildings to stand out from the mass of lesser buildings, many in the classical style, which surrounded them, and to be 'sermons in stone', or as Vaughan Hart describes them, 'foci of remembrance ... and emblems of death and resurrection'.

Owen Hopkins, author of *From the Shadows: The Architecture and Afterlife of Nicholas Hawksmoor,* sums up the enduring impact of his London churches: 'Colossal in scale, of brilliant white stone, stark and austere in design yet resonant with allusions to architecture distant in time and place, these churches still dominate their areas even as the city has grown around them.' Just as they sent powerful signals to their local inhabitants three centuries ago, so they continue to speak to us and to challenge us today.

Flaming urns, St Bride's Fleet Street. A signature feature of Hawksmoor, symbolising death and resurrection. (Stuart Vallis)

Above: The lantern and tower of Ely Cathedral, Cambridgeshire. The fourteenth-century octagonal lantern, tower and stair turrets find echoes in Hawksmoor's churches. (jcw1967, Flickr)

Right: The octagonal lantern at the top of the tower of St George-in-the-East. (Stuart Vallis)

3
Hawksmoor's City Church Spires

The list below includes all the City Church spires which may have been influenced by Hawksmoor, as well as those for which there is documentary evidence. They are listed in rough date order of the work on the spires (the main church buildings were all completed earlier). Their locations are given for those who might wish to visit and see them in situ.

All Hallows Bread Street: 1681–88, demolished 1877
Bread Street, EC4M 9AJ

St Mary Somerset: 1685–94, demolished 1869
5 Lambeth Hill, EC4V 4AG

St Andrew Holborn: 1684–86
5 St Andrew Street, EC4A 3AF

St Dunstan-in-the-East: 1695–1701
St Dunstan Hill, EC3R 5DD

St Augustine Watling Street: 1695–96, destroyed 1941
St Paul's Churchyard, EC4M 8AD

St Margaret Pattens: 1698–1702
Rood Lane, EC3M 1HS

St Bride's Fleet Street: 1701–04
Fleet Street, EC4Y 8AU

St Magnus the Martyr: 1703–06
Lower Thames Street, EC3R 6DN

St Edmund the King: 1706–07
Lombard Street, EC3V 9AN

St Vedast Foster Lane: 1709–12
4 Foster Lane, EC2V 6HH

St Michael Crooked Lane: 1709–14, demolished 1831
Martin Lane, Cannon Street, EC4R 0DP

St Stephen Walbrook: 1713–15
39 Walbrook, EC4N 8BN

St James Garlickhythe: 1713–17
Garlick Hill, EC4V 2AF

St Michael Paternoster Royal: 1713–17
College Hill, EC4R 2RL

St Michael Cornhill: 1715–22
St Michael's Alley: EC3V 9DS

4

Hawksmoor's London Churches

Having sketched the outline of Nicholas Hawksmoor's life, made reference to the social and political context in which he began his work, and given a brief account of some of the sources of his design repertoire and the influences upon his work, it is now time to examine in detail the six churches in London which he designed, and which still stand today. They lie in very different parts of the capital, the area of the East End amidst hamlets crowded with poor dwellings, where their ornament is simpler and more austere, and by contrast the well-to-do neighbourhoods of London's City and West End, where the ornament is richer.

We shall begin our journey beyond the East End, in Greenwich, with the parish church of St Alfege, and work our way westwards until we reach Westminster Abbey, whose towers are among Hawksmoor's last designs.

St Alfege Greenwich
Greenwich Church Street, SE10 9BJ

There has been a Christian church on this site for nearly a thousand years. The medieval foundation was dedicated to St Alfege, Archbishop of Canterbury, and reputedly marks the place where he was martyred in 1012. In the former thirteenth-century building King Henry VIII, born in Greenwich Palace, was baptised in 1491. Thomas Tallis, father of English Church music, played the organ here, and is buried beneath the east end of the church. However, in November 1710, a violent storm destroyed the church's roof and made the whole building unsafe for worship. So, the parish presented a petition to Parliament on 6 April 1711 for assistance. They asked for a sum of £6,000 from the Coal Tax to be assigned for its rebuilding. St Alfege's thus became the first of what the government hoped would

The east end of St Alfege, fronting the main road, and looking like a Roman temple. (Stuart Vallis)

be fifty new churches built during the reign of Queen Anne to serve London's growing population.

Hawksmoor designed a rectangular building with a flat ceiling and a small apse. The east front, facing the main highway, consists of a main portico in the Tuscan order with a central arch cutting through the broken frieze and pediment resting on two columns. Giant pilasters run round the sides of the church with projecting vestibules rising the full height of the building, and with open staircases leading to them. The 'bollards' at the east end, which mark off the curtilage of the church, are 4 feet tall in Portland limestone, and are carved with swags of drapery and the heads of putti, looking like fragments of a pagan temple reused for Christian purposes, just as Hawksmoor intended. From the road the building looks like a Roman temple, which is not surprising as Hawksmoor took inspiration from the Roman Temple of Bacchus at Baalbek (Heliopolis) in Lebanon, which he had reconstructed in a drawing from travel reports and eyewitness accounts.

The church was completed by 1714, and those involved in the work were:

Masons: Edward Strong and Edward Tufnell
Plasterers: James Ellis and James Hands
Joiner: Grinling Gibbons, Richard Jones, Joseph Wade, John Boson, and Thomas Darby
Painting around the altar: Sir James Thornhill

Above left: The four massive altars which define the curtilage of the church. (Stuart Vallis)

Above right: A detail of one of the altars, with carved cherubs and drapery. (Stuart Vallis)

Left: The south side of the church, showing the deeply recessed windows, large key stones, and the spire added later by John James in 1730. (Stuart Vallis)

Opposite: A view showing the giant pilasters and large central vestibule projection. (Stuart Vallis)

The rectangular flat ceiling resting on small corbels, upper galleries, and domed apse. (Stuart Vallis)

In order to save money, the tower of the old church was retained, and refaced in 1730 by another of the Commission's architects, John James, who added the steeple.

There were two churchyards, the later one re-laid as a garden and recreation ground called St Alfege Park.

Inside, the ceiling rises from shallow corbels, and pairs of giant columns flank the reredos within the apsidal east end. The walls around the altar were intended to be decorated with designs by Sir James Thornhill, an English painter, for which drawings survive. These were repainted by Glyn Jones following wartime damage.

During the Blitz the church was fire-bombed on 19 March 1941, and most of the original interior perished. The two Benefaction Boards hanging on the eastern walls, the first recording benefactions dating from 1558, and the second surmounted by the Royal Arms of Queen Anne, used to hang in the lobby of an internal staircase, and so were unharmed when the church was bombed.

During the war, the crypt was turned into an air-raid shelter, and in 1953 the church was restored by Sir Albert Richardson. The glass in the East Window is by Francis

The west gallery and organ. (Stuart Vallis)

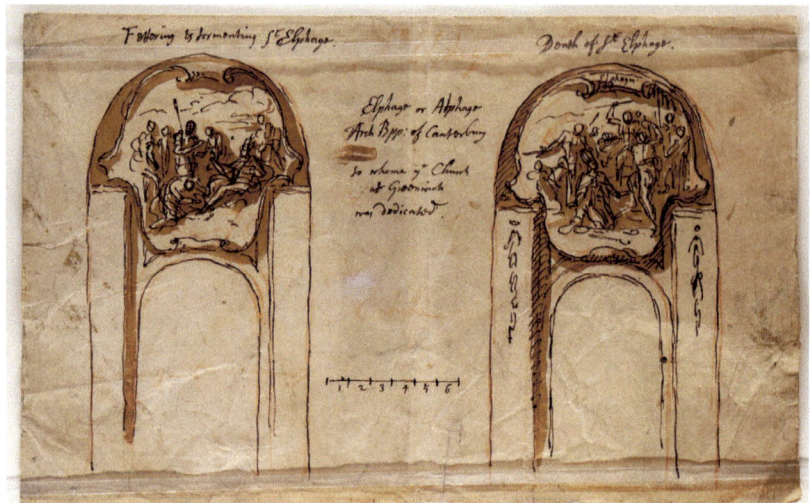

Sir James Thornhill's drawing for the frescoes surrounding the altar within the apse. (Stuart Vallis)

Above left: The right-hand Benefaction Board. (Stuart Vallis)

Above right: The left-hand Benefaction Board with the Royal Arms of Queen Anne. (Stuart Vallis)

H. Spear, installed in 1953, and shows the Risen Christ with St Alfege beneath him on the left and on the right Cardinal Morton, who was believed (mistakenly) to have been Vicar of the church before becoming Archbishop of Canterbury.

The interior was tastefully rebuilt using some of the old wood which survived the conflagration, such as the fine columns behind the altar, designed by Grinling Gibbons. The iron altar rails, the work of the French craftsman Jean Tijou, also survived the bombing. Although it is beautifully maintained, this is not the interior which Hawksmoor would have known. However, the exterior of the church looks much as it did in his time. He was working with a site and orientation determined by the original medieval church, and the highlight is undoubtedly the eastern exterior with its massive portico making it look like an antique temple standing in Greenwich High Street. What an extraordinary impact it must have made when it first opened for worship in 1714.

A view of the west end of the church and tower. (Stuart Vallis)

St Anne Limehouse
Three Colt Street, E14 7HA

Leaving the relative seclusion and charm of Greenwich, the next church is in the riverside hamlet of Limehouse, originally part of the vast parish of St Dunstan's Stepney. Its name comes from the lime kilns which had been established by the fourteenth century to serve the London building trade. The population of the area, largely engaged in seafaring and allied trades, expanded greatly in the seventeenth century, and this led to the demand for more places of worship, which resulted in the Fifty New Churches Act of 1711.

Surrounded by a grove of big leafy trees, but approached from the west by a narrow lane between eighteenth-century houses, one gains an impression of how

The west front and tower, facing a narrow lane with original houses, showing the entrance rotunda and dome. (Stuart Vallis)

contemporary visitors would have seen this monumental new building when it was finally consecrated in 1730. The tower rises massive and sculptural, dominating the neighbourhood, as Hawksmoor intended, growing out of the body of the church with a semi-circular projection at the base, incorporating the main doors. The upper part of the tower is rectangular and leads the eye to the arch of the bell-opening, which in turn leads up to the octagonal top of the tower, described by Pevsner, in *London Docklands* (Penguin, 1999, p. 144), as 'the equivalent perhaps of a medieval lantern, very Baroque in its changes of direction but with no sinuous flourishes at all'.

Ian Nairn, in *Nairn's London* (Penguin Books, 2014, p. 163), also comments, 'The octagonal top is a staccato crop of columns and obelisks, with everything set diagonal and at twenty degrees to everything else.'

Wide steps lead up to the west doors, and you enter under the cupola of the vestibule, domed and lit from arched upper windows. In an elevated niche is the nineteenth-century monument to Maria Charlesworth.

The sides of the church are stone-faced and plain, punctured by arched gallery windows, below which are square ones, and below these the crypt windows. The

The south side of the church, showing the massive height of the tower and deeply recessed windows in the plain south wall. (Stuart Vallis)

east end has an arched motif, and the vestries are topped with what Pevsner describes as 'brutal rectangular angle towers'. Jutting above the roofline they make a bold and aggressive statement.

The interior is arranged in a cruciform shape with a circular ceiling in the centre, and stone columns with Corinthian capitals.

After a disastrous fire in 1850, which destroyed the interior, the church was rebuilt by Philip Hardwick and John Morris, who also designed the font.

The glass in the East Window is by Charles Clutterbuck, a representation of the Crucifixion, with above it a representation of sky and cherubim withdrawing curtains. The crypt below the church has beautifully constructed vaulting in red brick and is full of atmosphere.

Above left: The octagonal steeple with golden ball and White Ensign, visible to shipping on the River Thames. (Stuart Vallis)

Above right: One of the two rooftop pavilions, looking aggressively modernist. (Stuart Vallis)

The south side of the church. (Stuart Vallis)

Above: The lunette with massive keystone at the east end of the church. (Stuart Vallis)

Left: The stone pyramid in the churchyard, dating from 1730, which may originally have been intended to stand on top of one of the pavilions. (Stuart Vallis)

Those responsible for the original work were:

Masons: Edward Strong and Edward Tufnell, Christopher Cass and Thomas Dunn
Carpenters: Robert Jelfe, James Grove, John James and John Meard
Joiners: Thomas Holden and John Balshaw
Carvers: Joseph Wade and Thomas Darby
Plasterer: Chrysostom Wilkins

Right: The interior of St Anne's Church, looking east. (Stuart Vallis)

Below left: The interior looking west, showing the organ gallery of 1856–57 by P. C. Hardwick. (Stuart Vallis)

Below right: The richly ornamented Corinthian columns and ceiling. (Stuart Vallis)

Right: The ceiling rose with cherubs. (Stuart Vallis)

Opposite: The circular entrance vestibule with the monument to Maria Charlesworth. (Stuart Vallis)

Below left: The font in neo-medieval style by Philip Hardwick, 1853. (Stuart Vallis)

Below right: The pulpit by Arthur Blomfield, 1856, carving by William Gibbs. (Stuart Vallis)

Above: Brick vaulting in the crypt. (Stuart Vallis)

Left: A part of the crypt showing old burial vaults, in the middle one for John Seaward, 1839. (Stuart Vallis)

Opposite: A view of the tower looking upwards. (Stuart Vallis)

In the churchyard there is an unusual pyramid, north-west of the church, panelled in stone and inscribed with 'The Wisdom of Solomon' in English and Hebrew. It dates from 1730 and may originally have been designed to sit on top of one of the square pavilions at the east end.

The church was named in honour of Queen Anne, who decreed that it should be a place where sea captains could register events at sea, such as deaths, and so gave the church the right to display the White Ensign. The clock was designed as a special maritime clock for shipping on the Thames, with a golden ball above for navigational purposes.

Christ Church Spitalfields
Commercial Street, E1 6LY

Moving further west to the very edge of the vast ancient parish of St Dunstan's Stepney, where the East End meets the City, is an area where Huguenots from France and Jews from Europe had settled, encouraged by the Protector Thomas Cromwell, and then by the Toleration Act of King William III.

Encouraged to assert the presence and authority of the Church of England in such a heterodox area, Hawksmoor started work on designing a suitably imposing building, and work began in 1714, but proceeded slowly. The church was finally consecrated in July 1729 at the enormous cost of £19,418.

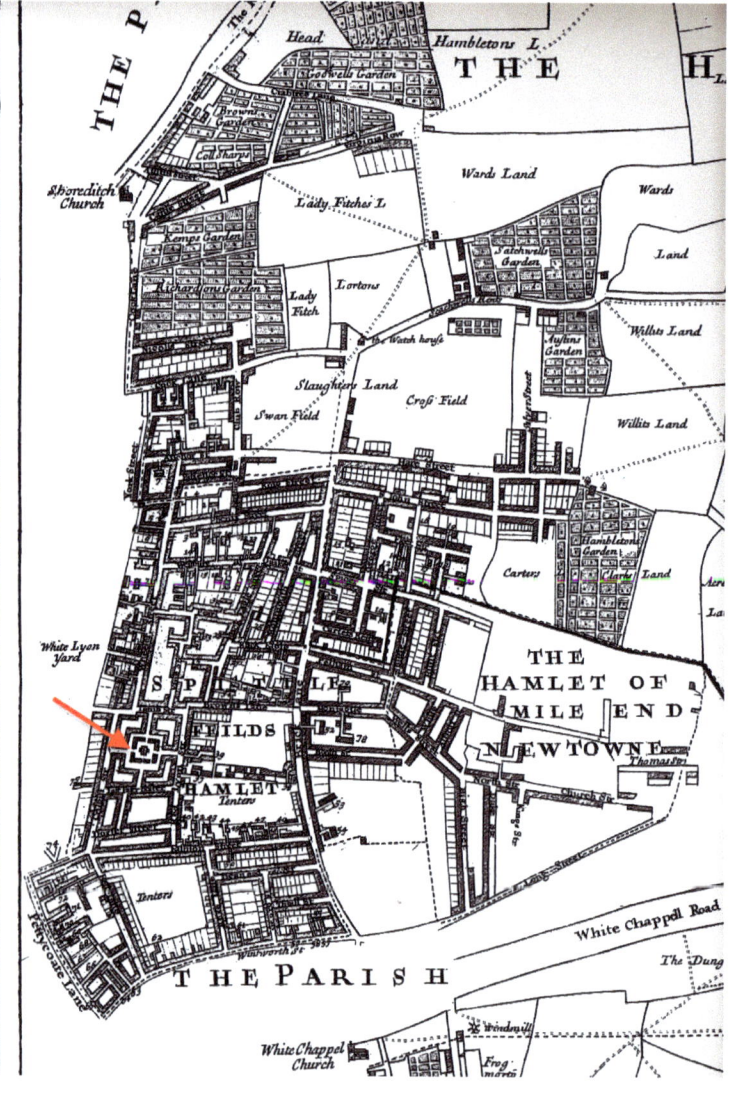

An early eighteenth-century map showing the hamlet of Spitalfields with its neat rows of streets, surrounded by fields and gardens. (Wikipedia Commons)

Those involved in the work were:

Mason: Thomas Dunn
Carpenters: James Grove and Samuel Worrall
Plasterer: Isaac Mansfield
Carvers: John Darby and Gervase Smith

The church sits on Commercial Street but is best seen from the west down Brushfield Street, where the massive tower and spire rears up above the eighteenth-century houses and dominates the streetscape. By the time Hawksmoor was beginning his

The majestic west end and tower of the church, looking down Brushfield Street. (Stuart Vallis)

design the Earl of Shaftsbury had written an influential letter attacking the designs of Sir Christopher Wren, including St Paul's Cathedral, Hampton Court, and by implication Blenheim Palace and the Fifty New Churches. The Baroque style was under attack and the more restrained Palladian style was in the ascendant. Hawksmoor disliked the Palladian camp, but here at Christ Church Spitalfields he made use of a prominent Palladian motif but on a vast scale, the Venetian window, an arched opening between two rectangular ones. It's tempting to think that it was Hawksmoor's gesture of defiance to his rivals. The north wall stands sheer opposite the brick terraces of Fournier Street, and on the south side the porthole windows that give light to the upper galleries echo those at Blenheim, and the arches are extended downwards to include the lower windows which give light to the aisles under the galleries.

The original houses of Fournier Street, just visible on the left, show how Christ Church dominated the streetscape when it was first built. (Stuart Vallis)

The south side of the church, with a slightly projecting series of five bays, indented windows with big keystones, and a doorway approached by a double staircase. (Stuart Vallis)

The interior looking west, with the splendid organ case of 1735 by Robert Bridge on a west gallery supported by fluted Corinthian columns. (Stuart Vallis)

In front of the tower is a lofty portico with four Tuscan columns and a semi-circular arch in the middle. Above the smaller final stage with its arched window rises the tall octagonal steeple, which looks more Gothic than classical, especially when it had its original decoration of crockets and small dormer windows.

Inside, the main space is rectangular, with Corinthian columns, and on the grand scale, with barrel vaults in the aisles, a flat ceiling, and a chancel separated by a series of four columns, forming a kind of screen. At the east end is a large Venetian window. There is a fine pulpit, communion rails and Royal Arms, and a magnificent

Above: The east end and chancel with large Venetian window, separated from the nave by a screen formed of freestanding columns and an architrave. (Stuart Vallis)

Right: The Royal Arms above the eastern screen, in Coade stone by William Croggan, *c.* 1820. (Stuart Vallis)

65

Left: The memorial to Edward Peck (d. 1736) by Thomas Dunn, the chief mason of the church, commemorating the vestry member who laid the foundation stone for the church. (Stuart Vallis)

Below left: The side arcade with tall columns and clerestory windows above. (Stuart Vallis)

Below right: The transverse barrel vault over the aisle with richly elaborate decoration. (Stuart Vallis)

organ case by Robert Bridge, 1735. At the east end are two important monuments, the one on the south side to Edward Peck Esq., died 19 June 1735, consisting of a bust on a sarcophagus with cherubs and a classical entablature. It was sculpted by Thomas Dunn, the chief mason, and erected in 1737. The inscription reads, 'He was one of the Commissioners for Building the fifty new churches, and in this corner laid the first stone of this Stately Fabrick Anno 1715.'

Opposite Peck is another monument, to Sir Robert Ladbroke, Knight and Alderman, President of Christ's Hospital, Lord Mayor MDCCXLVII (1747), who died on 31 October 1773. He stands in his eighteenth-century mayoral robes with the mace and sword of office lying on the ground behind him. The monument is by John Flaxman. Both monuments, and the chancel area, are currently hidden behind temporary modern screens.

By 1957, the church was nearly derelict, and was closed, but in 1976 The Friends of Christ Church Spitalfields was formed, and a major restoration programme was begun, which was completed by 2000. The full restoration of the interior, including the galleries, was finished in 2004.

Pevsner called the church 'ugly, in spite of all one's admiration for Hawksmoor's originality'. On the contrary, it is perhaps the most majestic and overpowering of all Hawksmoor's churches, and the twentieth-century restoration work has revealed Hawksmoor's building in all its splendour, raw power, and magnificence.

The font with bulbous shaft and oval bowl. (Stuart Vallis)

St George-in-the-East
4 Cannon Street Road, E1 0BH

Due south from the now smart and prosperous streets around Spitalfields is an area that feels more neglected, bisected by the busy road called The Highway. Driving along this road today, or travelling on the elevated Docklands Light Railway, you cannot fail to spot an extraordinary-looking church building, which Ian Nairn said was 'probably the hardest building to describe in London ... all the details ingested, fused together'. Owen Hopkins, in his *Nicholas Hawksmoor London Map*, comments, 'This is architecture as three-dimensional collage.'

Built to serve the eastern part of Wapping, inhabited by skilled artisans and those working in the docks along the Thames, the church was begun in 1715 and consecrated in 1729.

The exterior of the church, showing the tower with deep-set windows, and ending in an octagonal lantern. (Stuart Vallis)

An early drawing of St George's, showing the narrow platform in front of the church approached by two flights of stairs. This was later altered. (Stuart Vallis)

Those who worked on the building were:

    Masons: Edward Strong, Edward Tufnell, Christopher Cass
    Carpenters: James Grove and John Meard
    Plasterers: John and Chrysostom Wilkins
    Carvers: Joseph Wade and Thomas Darby

The cost of the building was £18,557.

You approach the church from an entrance on Cannon Street Road and are faced with a wide flight of steps leading to a platform. The tower rises before you, flanked by vestries, with deeply recessed windows. It is crowned with an octagonal lantern, reminiscent of medieval examples such as Boston parish church, and so with allusions to the Gothic style, but with buttresses topped off with round turrets in the style of Roman altars. Here again is an example of Hawksmoor playfully bringing together classical and medieval architectural forms.

At each side of the church there are entrances to two stair turrets elongated above the roof and finished with octagonal tops with small domes, a dramatic sight. The doors have heavy lintels and keystones, as do the lower nave windows, which give them an aggressive and menacing appearance.

Above left: The pepperpot towers which crown the stair turrets giving access to the galleries. (Stuart Vallis)

Above right: The octagonal top of the tower which is reminiscent of that on Ely Cathedral, but with buttresses crowned with Roman altars. (Stuart Vallis)

Left: One of the oversize austere doors on the south side, which originally gave access to the galleries. (Stuart Vallis)

The church was badly bombed in 1941, and then reconstructed after the war, when a smaller church space was created inside the original outer walls. The vaults were turned into a hall, and a rectory and flats were also included within the walls. The 1960s church retained Hawksmoor's apse, with the later mosaic panels of 1880. There is a handsome eighteenth-century font with an octagonal bowl, and an interesting memorial on one of the pillars in the south aisle, a tablet

Above: Three windows punched into the south wall, looking both menacing and aggressive. (Stuart Vallis)

Right: Interior view of the apse, showing the eighteenth-century plasterwork and mosaic panels of 1880. (Stuart Vallis)

of brushed steel commemorating the fire bombing of the church on 16 April 1941, incorporating a painting by Peter Bedford. The inscription reads:

> This painting commemorates the destruction of the original interior of this church by incendiary bomb during the Blitz.
>
> Painted some fifty years later and presented by the artist Peter Bedford who as a member of the Pacifist Service Units was fire watching on the church roof on the night when the bomb fell.
> Remember before God the destruction and horror of war
> Pray and work for peace and reconciliation in our world.
> Peter Bedford Architect and Artist
> Died on 27th April 1998
> Give thanks for his courage and greatness of Spirit.

Another memorial on the east wall of the south aisle commemorates a former rector, Alexander Solomon, Rector 1958–79, 'whose vision inspired the rebuilding of this church'.

Above left: The glazed centre of the west wall, installed in the restoration of 1960–64, with a view of the tower beyond. (Stuart Vallis)

Above right: The eighteenth-century font with octagonal bowl on a baluster stem. (Stuart Vallis)

Above left: The memorial to Peter Bedford, architect and artist (d. 1998), which also commemorates the destruction of the church during the London Blitz on 16 April 1941. (Stuart Vallis)

Above right: The memorial to the Revd Alexander Solomon, Rector 1958–79, who inspired the rebuilding of the church. (Stuart Vallis)

Right: The powerful exterior of the apse at the east end. (Stuart Vallis)

The churchyard was laid out as a public garden in 1886 and gives the church a much more spacious setting than it would originally have had. Many picturesque headstones line the walls, and in the middle is a prominent monument in memory of Mrs Sarah Raine, d. 1725, Mrs Elizabeth Raine, d. 1732, and Henry Raine, brewer, d. 1738. He was born in 1679 and made his fortune in brewing. In 1719, he built a charity school in Wapping, providing education for fifty boys and fifty girls, who went on to apprenticeships and into service. He was a key figure in the creation of the parish of St George-in-the-East in 1729, linking the schools he founded with the new parish.

The monument consists of a square pyramid on a two-stage base, with on the south face an achievement of arms and on the north face a relief of a semi-reclining woman.

While standing in the churchyard, under the trees, you can look back at the sheer east wall, with the pepperpots and massive tower looming above, a strange mixture of classical and Gothic, 'bursting upwards from the ground', and marvel at the weirdness of invention which Hawksmoor conjured up in this part of London.

Above: The east end of the church, with a view of the Raine monument (1738) in the churchyard. (Stuart Vallis)

Opposite: The octagonal tower juxtaposed with the pepperpot staircase tower. (Stuart Vallis)

St Mary Woolnoth, City of London
King William Street, EC3V 9AY

Moving further west, into the prosperous environs of the City of London, the setting is quite a contrast to that of the previous church in Wapping. Here, at the junction of Lombard Street and King William Street, Hawksmoor was presented with a very constricted site, closed in by buildings and streets on three sides. When the church was first built there was no open space in the front as there is now, and the parish was a maze of small lanes and alleys.

An exterior view of the west front, showing the semi-circular steps leading up to a round-headed doorway, and the extraordinary tower, looking like two separate towers merged together to produce an effect of great strength and solidity. (Stuart Vallis)

Along Lombard Street there was an open space still known as the Stocks Market, where offenders were chained and pelted with rotten fruit and vegetables. Beyond the Wallbrook lay Poultry and Scalding Alley where feathers were burnt off poultry, and between Cornhill and Lombard Street was an area known as Change where the new coffee houses were doing a roaring trade alongside the many inns selling beer and gin.

Into this noisesome and bustling environment Hawksmoor was tasked with inserting his new church. The old medieval church had become so ruinous that the parishioners didn't dare to enter. In 1711, they presented a petition to the House of Commons, and in 1715 made a request that it should be included in the Fifty New Churches Scheme. Rebuilding began in 1716, and Hawksmoor combined mathematical regularity, squareness, and weight with his love of all things Roman to produce one of the most original churches in the City.

Those involved in the work were:

Mason:	Thomas Dunn
Plasterer:	Chrysostom Wilkins
Joiner:	Gabriel Appleby
Carpenters:	William Seager, Thomas Denning, James Grove and John Meard

The church cost the extravagant sum of £16,542 to build.

Low external doorways on either side of the tower, originally giving access to the galleries, the arch ornamented with playful faces of cherubs. (Stuart Vallis)

The tower with its twin turrets is broader than it is long, giving an impression of strength and monumentality, the base with strong rustications leading to the band of small square windows, above which are three groups of columns leading the eye upwards to the two turrets, which would have been visible over the rooftops.

The north wall has deeply recessed and rusticated niches containing Ionic columns, which gave interest and solemnity to this view of the building while stopping noise penetrating inside.

The crypt and platform of the church were used in 1897 to create a booking hall for the former Underground station, the facade of which conceals a vestry at the south-east end with a Venetian window.

The north side of the church, ornamented with heavily rusticated blank frames, each with two columns resting on protruding sills. Below are the crypt windows with Hawksmoor's outsize keystones. (Stuart Vallis)

The central square space, framed by four groups of three giant Corinthian columns. The big semi-circular windows allow light to pour into the church. The design is reminiscent of the Egyptian hall described by Vitruvius. (Stuart Vallis)

The interior is modelled on a Roman atrium, nearly square, with three Corinthian columns in each angle and with semi-circular windows above. Ian Nairn comments, 'It is a square inside a square, the inner top lit with great lunettes concentrating everything down towards the centre and you in it.'

The interior was altered by William Butterfield in 1875–76, and although much of the woodwork is original, the galleries were dismantled and the front panels set against the walls. Only the west organ gallery survives. The splendidly bulging pulpit is original as is the communion table, and the baldacchino with its twisted columns makes a rich and satisfying focal point for the interior.

This view of the reredos shows the high square space of the interior. (Stuart Vallis)

Another interior view, showing the Baldacchino, pulpit, chandelier and Royal Coat of Arms. (Stuart Vallis)

The fine baldacchino with twisted columns, and an elaborately ornamented canopy, made by John Meard and carved by Gabriel Appleby, and framing the Commandment Boards. The Communion Table has a marble top and is dated *c.* 1720. (Stuart Vallis)

Above left: The bulbous front of the pulpit, made by Darby and Smith and inlaid by Appleby. (Stuart Vallis)

Above right: The tester of the pulpit echoes the shape of Hawksmoor's ceiling. (Stuart Vallis)

Right: The monument to the slave owner and hymn writer John Newton (d. 1807), north wall. (Stuart Vallis)

On the north wall is a wall tablet to John Newton, the hymn-writer. The inscription reads:

> JOHN NEWTON
> CLERK.
> ONCE AN INFIDEL AND LIBERTINE,
> A SERVANT OF SLAVES IN AFRICA,
> WAS,
> BY THE RICH MERCY
> OF OUR LORD AND SAVIOUR
> JESUS CHRIST.
> PRESERVED, RESTORED, PARDONED,
> AND APPOINTED TO PREACH THE FAITH
> HE HAD LONG LABOURED TO DESTROY.
>
> -------------
>
> HE MINISTERED
> NEAR XVI YEARS AS CURATE AND VICAR
> OF *OLNEY IN BUCKS*,
> AND XXVIII YEARS AS RECTOR
> OF THESE UNITED PARISHES.
>
> -------------
>
> ON FEBY THE FIRST MDCCL, HE MARRIED
> MARY,
> DAUGHTER OF THE LATE GEORGE CATLETT,
> OF *CHATHAM, KENT*.
> WHOM HE RESIGNED
> TO THE LORD WHO GAVE HER,
> ON DECR THE XVTH MDCCXC.
>
> The above Epitaph was written by the Deceased who directed it to be inscribed on a Plain Marble Tablet.
>
> -------------
>
> He died on Decr the 21st 1807. Aged 82 years, and his mortal Remains are deposited in the Vault beneath this Church.

In the south-east corner by the entrance to the vestry is the original mechanism of the clock with a quote from 'The Waste Land' by T. S. Eliot:

... Flowed up the hill and down King William Street
To where St Mary Woolnoth kept the hours.

Above left: The preserved original mechanism of the clock, the dials inscribed with the names of the churchwardens at the time of the repair in 1786. (Stuart Vallis)

Above right: Detail of cherubs over the external gallery door. (Stuart Vallis)

Right: Detail of the church clock mechanism. (Stuart Vallis)

St George's Bloomsbury
Bloomsbury Way, WC1A 2SA

All of Hawksmoor's prodigious inventiveness and his marshalling of eclectic stylistic references come together in the last of his surviving London churches, begun in 1716 and completed in 1731. Here, in a single composition are brought together the portico of the Pantheon, the facade of Christopher Wren's Sheldonian, and the Mausoleum of Halicarnassus repurposed as a spire.

The new parish of St George's was carved out of the parish of St Giles-in-the-Fields in the early eighteenth century to serve the more fashionable area of Bloomsbury, but again Hawksmoor had to deal with a constricted site hemmed in by houses.

The church on its constricted site as seen from Bloomsbury Way, with its grand six-column portico, and on the west side the tower with its stepped spire. (Stuart Vallis)

The land for the church had been purchased from the widow of Lord John Russell and consisted of a north-south rectangle. This meant that Hawksmoor had to try to solve the problem of an east-west orientation on a north-south site.

In defiance of the constricted site Hawksmoor created what Pevsner described as 'the most grandiose of London's 18th century church fronts', the six-column portico, modelled on the Temple of Jupiter at Baalbek in Lebanon, and originally intended as a show front, as the main entrances were at the top of staircases on the north and south sides of the tower. H. S. Goodhart-Rendel comments, 'It looks like one of the Temples of Roman Londinium preserved and adapted for Christian use.' The tower is placed on the west side of the church for maximum visibility, and its final stage is based on the Roman historian Pliny's description of

The spire of St George's, modelled on the Mausoleum of Halicarnassus, and crowned with the figure of King George I. There are lion and unicorn supporters at the base. (Stuart Vallis)

the Mausoleum of Halicarnassus, one of the Seven Wonders of the World. It was topped with a statue of King George I dressed in a Roman toga, to emphasise the authority of the Hanoverian succession, with at the base of the pyramid fighting lions and unicorns symbolising the end of the First Jacobite Rebellion, the fight for the Crown between England and Scotland. These figures would have been well known at the time because of the popular nursery rhyme:

> The lion and the unicorn were fighting for the crown,
> The lion beat the unicorn all around the town.

The figure of the king accompanied by these exotic beasts was, however, the object of contemporary ridicule, as the following verse by Horace Walpole demonstrates:

> When Henry the Eighth left the Pope in the lurch,
> The Protestants made him the head of the church;
> But George's good subjects, the Bloomsbury people,
> Instead of the Church, made him head of the steeple.

The altar and baldacchino in the eastern apse. (Stuart Vallis)

Inside, the plan is a square atrium, lit by a clerestory with north and south aisles divided from the central space by pairs of columns supporting an entablature. The original reredos of Cuban mahogany with its open pediment on Corinthian columns is in its eastern niche, with the ceiling decoration of winged cherubs in clouds above mitres and crosiers by Isaac Mansfield, who also made the plasterwork centre flower in the main ceiling. The font, now sited near the south entrance, is dated 1726. Anthony Trollope, the Victorian novelist, was baptised in it on 18 May 1815.

The original galleries were demolished in 1871, but when the church underwent a major restoration in 2002–06 the north and south galleries were reinstalled, and the church was returned to its original east-west orientation.

The north side of the interior, with pairs of columns joined by an arch. Behind them are galleries, originally intended for the use of the Duke of Bedford. (Stuart Vallis)

Gin Lane by William Hogarth, 1750/1. This engraving is Hogarth's satirical comment on what he saw as London's moral and physical degeneration, which characterised the area around the Church of St George in Bloomsbury, whose distinctive tower appears in the background. Hogarth appears to be saying that in spite of the Fifty New Churches Act, squalor and drunkenness, death and disease still abound, leading to a breakdown of the moral and social order which neither the government nor the monarch have been able to reverse. This engraving is an ironic and posthumous verdict on the ambitious church-building programme of which Nicholas Hawksmoor was the chief architect and guiding spirit.

Above: The elaborate decoration on the keystone of the north arch. (Stuart Vallis)

Right: The north frontage of the church, looking onto Barter Street, stone-faced, 'very secular and palatial' (Pevsner). (Stuart Vallis)

The north face of the church is stone-faced with Hawksmoor's signature deeply recessed windows and outsize keystones. The look is 'secular and palatial'. This side of the church is reached by a narrow passage on the west side of the church, which, as Ian Nairn points out, 'distils that great man's imagination in a more personal and direct way than any of his better buildings'. On the left-hand side of the building the gap between the church and the neighbouring buildings narrows, the passage dives down, turns a corner, then goes up again. In a moment of great drama, you emerge onto Little Russell Street, where you can see the rear elevation of St George's towering above you. Nairn was absolutely right, and you can still experience that feeling of surprise today.

The Final Designs

St George's Bloomsbury was built at great expense, as were all Hawksmoor's churches, which is one of the reasons why only twelve of the commission's fifty churches were ever constructed. Two Hawksmoor churches, of which little remain, were collaborations with another architect, John James, perhaps brought in to try to

Left: St John Horsleydown, demolished after the Second World War. (Architectural Press Archive/RIBA Collections)

Below: St Luke's Old Street, with a fluted obelisk crowning the tower. (Wikipedia Commons)

mitigate Hawksmoor's extravagance. St John Horsleydown, 175 Tower Bridge Road, SE1 2AH (1726–33), was demolished after it was bombed in the Second World War; and only the steeple survives of St Luke's Old Street, 161 Old Street, EC1V 9NG (1727–33). St Luke's was a more modest building, with a fluted obelisk crowning the tower. It remains a splendid reminder of Hawksmoor's interest in funeral and memorial iconography, pointing to the heavens as a sign of Resurrection.

In spite of his obsession with the Classical world, Hawksmoor was interested in working in a variety of styles to make his buildings authentic and timeless, and as a result, as already noted, he experimented with the Gothic style. Between 1716 and 1720 he supervised repairs to Beverley Minster, and his work at All Souls College, Oxford (1716–35), shows that he was concerned to preserve medieval fabric and to design in a style sympathetic to the architectural context.

The two west towers of the abbey, begun by Hawksmoor in 1735 and completed in 1745, with Gothic features combined with the Baroque open pediments above the circular openings. Much of the carving was done by Sir Henry Cheere. (Stuart Vallis)

93

A view of the towers showing the three-light bell openings with ogee hoods and crockets. They convincingly complete the medieval west front of the abbey. (Stuart Vallis)

His final work, not finished until after his death, was the completion of the medieval frontage of Westminster Abbey, 20 Deans Yard, SW1P 3PA, which was begun in 1722 and finished in 1745.

Building on the experience of his earlier Gothic work, he completed the Perpendicular front of the abbey up to the level of the main wall headings, and then finished it off with an entablature, which was a base for his own additions, the two west towers. These towers, with canopies over the clock faces giving a classical element to the design, have a medieval feel about them, and may have been modelled on the late fourteenth-century west towers of Beverley Minster, where he had supervised repairs.

The large three-light bell openings are in a Perpendicular style, and the open-work parapet between the polygonal pinnacles is based on that formerly on Henry VII's Chapel. Pevsner calls the finished result 'plausibly medieval', and it is undoubtedly true that his sympathetic completion of the west front of the abbey has given it an iconic look, instantly recognised, even though few people today will know of its author. Hawksmoor, with his retiring and unostentatious character, would have been ruefully amused.

However, in spite of the eclipse of his fame for two centuries after his death, his reputation has been reassessed and rehabilitated in the twentieth century, partly through scholarly research, partly through the restoration of his churches, and partly through the notoriety conferred by the publication of Peter Ackroyd's novel *Hawksmoor*.

The monumentality of his architecture, his instinctive understanding of the way light falls over masonry, creating shapes and shadows, and his playful use of a wide range of eclectic references and styles appeals to contemporary architects, and continually surprises those who encounter his buildings for the first time, with a mixture of shock and wonder, the 'Terror and Magnificence' which Ackroyd put into the mouth of the Hawksmoor doppelgänger in his novel.

Kerry Downes has aptly summed up the appeal and power of Nicholas Hawksmoor's surviving London churches:

> The strangeness of many of Hawksmoor's formal devices has found recognition only in the present century's exploration of the subconscious. Ultimately the quality and character of his work cannot be put into prose. Its language is the one he knew best and knew as few other English architects have known: the eloquence of stone.

It's a compelling invitation to go and visit his London churches for yourself.

A Chronology of Nicholas Hawksmoor

1662   Born, probably in early 1662, at East Drayton, Nottinghamshire.
Worked as a clerk for Samuel Mellish, JP and Deputy Lieutenant for Yorkshire.

c.1679	Began work as a clerk to Sir Christopher Wren.
1683	Employed as Deputy Surveyor to Wren at Winchester Palace.
1689	Appointed Clerk of Works at William III's palace at Kensington.
1691–1712	Assisted Wren with work on St Paul's Cathedral.
1698–1735	Clerk of Works at Greenwich Hospital.
1699	Began work assisting Sir John Vanbrugh at Castle Howard, Yorkshire.
1702	Remodelling of the exterior of Easton Neston, Northamptonshire.
1705–16	Assistant surveyor to Vanbrugh at Blenheim Palace.
1711	One of the two surveyors appointed to carry out the Fifty New Churches Act.
1712	Clarendon Building, Oxford.
1712–14	St Alfege Greenwich, London.
1714–29	Christ Church Spitalfields, London.
1714–30	St Anne's Limehouse, London.
1715	Appointed Clerk of Works at Whitehall, Westminster, and St James.
1715–29	St George's-in-the-East, London.
1716–27	St Mary Woolnoth, London.
1716–31	St George's Bloomsbury, London.
1716–35	All Souls College, Oxford: north quadrangle, hall, buttery, and Codrington Library.
1721	Vanbrugh made Hawksmoor his deputy as Comptroller of the Works.
1722	Took over as architect in charge of work at Blenheim Palace.
1722–45	Designed the west towers of Westminster Abbey.
1723	Succeeded Wren as Surveyor to Westminster Abbey.
1729–36	Mausoleum at Castle Howard.
1736	Died of gout on 25 March at his house on Millbank. He is buried at St Botolph's, Shenley, Hertfordshire.